A History of the Papacy

by
Fr Nicholas Schofield

All booklets are published thanks to the generous support of the members of the Catholic Truth Society

CATHOLIC TRUTH SOCIETY
PUBLISHERS TO THE HOLY SEE

Contents

Introduction

When the Pope appears at his study window each Sunday to pray the Angelus with pilgrims, he is given many reminders that he is the Successor of St Peter. To his right is the great basilica built over the Apostle's tomb. In front of him the obelisk which once stood in Nero's circus and may have witnessed St Peter's martyrdom. In the distance, perched on the Janiculum hill, is San Pietro in Montorio, an alternative site of his crucifixion. Finally, below him, are the crowds filling the piazza, surrounded by Bernini's colonnade, which open like a pair of arms to embrace the world. The Petrine ministry involves acting not only as bishop of Rome but as 'Supreme Pontiff of the Universal Church'.

However, the story of the papacy begins not in the Vatican but the village of Caesarea Philippi. Jesus was on his way to Jerusalem, where he would be put to death, and asked His disciples, 'Who do you say I am?' Peter made his sublime confession of faith: 'You are the Christ, the son of the living God'. The Lord replied, 'You are Peter, and on this rock I will build my Church' (Mt 16: 13-20).

Peter, the simple fisherman from Galilee, far from perfect, was chosen as the leader of the Apostles, the visible head of the Church. There are many signs in the Gospels that Peter was given special prominence: he is named first in lists of the Twelve (e.g. Mt 10:1, Mk 3: 16) and in the group of three disciples who witnessed the Transfiguration (Mk 9: 1-7) and Jesus' agony in the garden (Mk 14: 37). On several occasions he asked questions on behalf of the others (e.g. Lk 12: 41) and, although John reached the empty tomb first, he allowed Peter to enter first (Jn 20: 3-10). On the day of Pentecost Peter was the first to speak to the crowds – in effect the first papal utterance (Acts 2: 14-41)

The *Acts of the Apostles* give many details of the first pontificate. St Peter is shown curing a lame man at the 'Beautiful Gate' of the Temple (Acts 3: 1-26), investigating the fraud of Ananias and Sapphira (Acts 5: 1-11) and answering Simon Magus, who tried to 'purchase' the Holy Spirit (Acts 8: 9-24). Initially reluctant to baptise uncircumcised Gentiles, he spoke in their favour at the Council of Jerusalem (Acts 15: 7-11) and worked as a missionary in Gentile areas. An early tradition records him as first bishop of Antioch and up until the 1960s there was a feast in the universal calendar of St Peter's Chair at Antioch (22 February).

Together with St Paul, St Peter is remembered as the founder of the Roman Church – the two Apostles acting as a Christian version of Romulus and Remus, the mythical founders of the city. There is no explicit mention in Scripture of St Peter living and dying in Rome. However, the Apostle's first letter mentions 'Babylon', a codename used for Rome by early Christians (1 Pet 5: 13), and the Gospel written by St Mark, thought to be one of St Peter's assistants, was written for the Christians of Rome. Moreover, the testimony of early Christian writers such as St Clement, St Ignatius of Antioch and St Irenaeus all link Rome with the closing years of St Peter's life.

A number of Roman traditions suggest the fisherman's presence at the heart of the Empire. He is said to have lived with Aquila and Priscilla (mentioned in Acts 18: 2) on the Aventine, near the site of the church of Santa Prisca, and with the Senator Pudens, who may have had a British wife, 'Claudia Britannica'. The altar that he supposedly used in this house is enshrined at the Lateran. His converts included the martyrs St Nereus and St Achilleus and during times of persecution he often hid in the catacombs of Sant'Agnese, where a seat carved out of the rock was long venerated as his throne and where he is said to have baptised. A small chapel on the Appian Way marks the spot where St Peter is said to have met Christ as he was trying to flee from Rome one day. The astonished apostle asked: *Domine, quo vadis?* (Lord, where are you going?), to which the answer came, *Eo Romam iterum crucifigi* (I go to Rome to be crucified anew). St Peter was thus given the strength to return to the city and face crucifixion during the persecution of Nero around the year 64.

From Christ to Charlemagne

The First Popes

The first successors of St Peter were often obscure figures. The majority are honoured as saints and five of them appear in the First Eucharistic Prayer (Roman Canon): SS Linus (c.66-c.78), Cletus or Anacletus (c.79-c.91), Clement (c.91-c.101), Sixtus (that is, the sixth Pope after St Peter, c.116-125) and Cornelius (251-53). For many of these early popes our main source is the sixth century *Liber Pontificalis*, which lists their names in chronological order but often with inaccurate dates.

The papacy had not yet developed the bureaucratic structures of later centuries. However, there is little doubt that Christians recognised the bishop of Rome as having a unique authority. St Clement I (c.91 – c.101) wrote a famous letter to the church in Corinth around 95, the first surviving example of the bishop of Rome intervening in affairs beyond his own city. St Ignatius, himself a successor of St Peter as bishop of Antioch, spoke a few years later of the Church of Rome 'presiding' over the other churches. Another early Church Father, St Irenaeus, wrote at the end of the second century that with the

Roman church, 'because of its superior origin, all the churches must agree, that is, all the faithful in the whole world, and it is in her that the faithful everywhere have maintained the apostolic tradition'.

Together with the rest of the Christian community, the first popes belonged to a religion that was officially proscribed and faced persecution, although this tended to be sporadic and often local in character: it would be an exaggeration to imagine the first Christians spending all their lives hiding in the catacombs. But imprisonment and death remained a constant threat and several Popes are honoured as martyrs. St Clement is said to have been exiled to the Crimea and thrown into the sea with a heavy anchor, while St Sixtus II (257-58) was beheaded along with his deacons.

During this period the popes did much work organising the Roman Church. St Fabian (236-50), for example, divided the city into seven districts, placing a deacon in charge of each. The prestige of the papacy also grew as it battled heresy and addressed theological debates. St Pius I (c.142 – c.155) condemned Marcion of Pontus, who rejected the Old Testament and claimed that Christ was the son of 'the good God' as distinct from the God of the Jews.

The first Latin pope, St Victor I (189–98), insisted that the whole Church should observe Easter on the Sunday following Passover, as was the custom in Rome, rather than on Passover Day itself (the so-called Quartodeciman date), as was the usage in the East. Any churches that refused to do this would be excluded from communion, earning the pontiff the rebuke of St Irenaeus. Like his predecessors he also condemned various heretics and even secured the release of Christians condemned to the mines of Sardinia by writing to Marcia, the Christian mistress of the Emperor Commodus. The papacy was growing in influence, even if it was not formally accepted by the Roman Empire. St Callistus I (217-22) had to deal with the negative effects of this rising profile. He faced the first anti-pope, St Hippolytus (217-35), and was murdered in Trastevere by a pagan mob that resented the Church's power.

The Conversion of Constantine

The fourth century started off badly for the Church, with the bloody persecution sparked off by the Emperor Diocletian's *Edict against Christians* (303), during which over half of the martyrs of the early Church suffered. However, the status of Christians within the Empire was to dramatically improve within a decade. Realising that the Roman Empire had grown too large for one man to rule effectively, Diocletian created four administrative regions to be governed by two Caesars and two Augusti (deputy emperors). The Empire was further divided into sections called dioceses, a term which would later be used by the Church. As might be expected, disagreements soon arose among the different emperors. In 312 Constantine attributed victory against his rival Maxentius to Jesus Christ, who appeared in a dream and then in the sky through the sign of the cross.

Although Constantine was only baptised years later on his deathbed, the Church immediately benefited from his favour. Constantine sponsored the building of a basilica over the shrine of St Peter on the Vatican hill and apparently helped dig the foundations himself, filling twelve baskets with earth to symbolise the apostles. He also gave to St Miltiades (311-14) the former palace of the Laterani family, which became the official papal residence and the site of his cathedral, St John Lateran. Other churches were erected and the Christian community began to rely increasingly on the income from its property and benefactions.

Constantine's conversion also added a new dimension that would dominate subsequent centuries – the relationship between the Church and State, between Pope and Emperor. The potential for conflict became immediately apparent when Constantine took upon it himself to call a Council at Nicaea to examine the teachings of Arius, who denied Christ's Divinity. Pope St

Silvester I (314-35) was invited but, given his old age, sent two representatives in his place. The resulting profession of faith, which stressed that the Son was 'consubstantial' *(homoousios)* with the Father, is still recited at Sunday Mass. However Arianism continued to cause great divisions. In an effort to restore peace and unity, Constantine was persuaded to exile St Athanasius of Alexandria, the great scourge of the Arians. The papacy soon got involved and in 355 Constantius (one of Constantine's sons) exiled Pope Liberius (352-66) and appointed the anti-pope Felix II (355-65) in his place. For several years two popes were present in Rome, one at the Lateran (Liberius), the other on the Via Aurelia (Felix), each claiming to have imperial sanction as bishop of Rome.

Constantine had also moved his capital to Constantinople, which he declared to be the 'new Rome' and a rival centre of ecclesiastical power. A Council was held there in 381 and tried, amongst other things, to establish that the bishop of Constantinople should be second only to the bishop of Rome. In response, St Damasus I (366-84) underlined that the Roman primacy was based on St Peter. With the absence of the emperor, Rome lost its political centrality but it could now truly become the city of the popes.

St Leo the Great

St Leo (440-61), the first pope to be called 'the Great', was elected *in absentia* in 440 while he was working in Gaul. As well as being a gifted theologian, he made it his mission to underline the Roman primacy, formulating what his predecessors had understood and practised. He acted strongly against the Monophysite heresy, which held that Christ had one nature. When the bishop of Constantinople dismissed a heretical monk called Eutyches, Leo wrote a statement of the Church's orthodox belief, that Christ is one person with two distinct natures (human and divine) – the so-called 'Tome of Leo'. A Council called by the Emperor at Ephesus in 449 rejected the 'Tome' but the Pope held another Council at Chalcedon two years later, which adopted Leo's profession as dogma. 'This is the faith of the Apostles', the bishops declared, 'Peter has spoken through the voice of Leo'.

Leo also showed much courage as the old order collapsed around him, persuading Attila the Hun not to plunder Rome in 452. Although he failed to save the city from another invader, Gaiseric the Vandal, in 455, Leo helped rebuild the city's churches.

The Byzantine Period

Following the fall of the Roman Empire, the resulting power vacuum in the Italian peninsula was filled by

Odoacer the German and Theodoric the Ostrogoth. In 534 the Byzantine Emperor, Justinian, tried to reconquer the western provinces of the Roman Empire and established the Exarchate of Ravenna, stretching across Italy.

Despite the shifting balance of power and the rising threat of another Germanic people, the Lombards, Rome remained loyal to Byzantium until the mid eighth century. On election, the name of the new pope was sent, together with tribute, to the emperor or the exarch in Ravenna for confirmation. This could lead to long delays – thirteen months in the case of Boniface V (619-25). The close link with the East was further reflected in the many items of papal paraphernalia, used into modern times, which are said to have originated in Byzantium: the triple crown (tiara), the *sedia gestatoria* (a portable throne on which the pontiff was carried) and the *flabella* (fans of ostrich feathers, carried on either side of the pope). Relations between Constantinople and Rome were often strained not only by political disagreements but theological controversies. In reality, the pope had a great deal of freedom but it was felt that imperial support was needed against the Lombards, who not only threatened Rome but subscribed to the heresy of Arianism.

The most famous pope of this 'Byzantine period' was St Gregory 'the Great' (590-504). He was born into a distinguished Roman family with close connections to the

Papacy; indeed, his great-grandfather was St Felix III (483-92, a widower at the time of election) and he was also related to St Agapitus I (535-36). Gregory was the first monk to ascend the throne of Peter, having converted his family home on the Caelian into a monastery, but had also been employed in the papal service, spending some time as a diplomat in Constantinople. Referring to himself as *servus servorum Dei* (servant of the servants of God), Pope Gregory did much to reorganise the lands belonging to the papacy (the 'patrimony of Peter'), tighten church discipline and liturgical practice and, like St Leo the Great, prevent Rome from being sacked, this time by King Agilulf the Lombard (593). Familiar with the ways of the East, he asserted the Roman primacy in his dealings with the Emperor and, like his predecessor Pelagius II (579-90), criticised the Patriarch of Constantinople's adoption of the title 'Ecumenical Patriarch'.

St Gregory is best remembered in the English-speaking world for his missionary zeal and the sending of St Augustine and a band of monks to the distant kingdom of Kent, arriving there in 597. It was the first time that a Roman pontiff had directly sponsored the evangelisation of a pagan nation. According to the often-told story, Gregory had once encountered English slaves being sold in a Roman market and commented *Non Angli sed angeli* (not Angles but angels).

The English came to have a great devotion to Rome and the office of the pope. Indeed, Christian Canterbury was established as a Kentish version of Rome – the new cathedral, like the Lateran, was dedicated as Christ Church, and a monastery was built outside the walls in honour of St Peter and St Paul. As a sign of his communion with Rome, Gregory sent St Augustine the pallium, which even to this day appears on the coat of arms of the Archbishops of Canterbury (as well as Westminster). Many Anglo-Saxons, including royalty, subsequently made the pilgrimage to Rome and it was the English Kings who began the custom of raising money for the papacy through 'Peter's pence.' Moreover, when English monks such as St Boniface helped bring the Gospel to Germany and other parts of northern Europe, they took with them this love for Peter. As Eamon Duffy has commented, 'for the newly Christian people of the barbarian north, the authority of the papacy would be understood, not as the contested precedence of the senior Patriarch in the ancient seat of Empire, but as the charism of the key-bearer. Rome was the place where Peter had been buried, where he still dwelt, and where he spoke through the living voice of his successor.'[1]

As well as seeing the expansion of the Church in the West, the seventh century saw the further disintegration

---

[1] Eamon Duffy, *Saints and Sinners, A History of the Popes* (1997), 56-57

of the former Roman Empire. Slavic tribes such as the
Avars took control of the Balkans, while the Persians
swept through the Near East, taking Antioch, Damascus
and Jerusalem and carrying off the True Cross. Soon after
the defeat of the Persians by the Emperor – and the
recovery of the relic – the rise of Islam definitively
altered the religious geography of the Mediterranean and
wiped away many ancient centres of Christianity.

In the face of these threats, a close cooperation between
Pope and Emperor might have been expected. However,
serious tensions remained. Many of the Emperor's subjects
did not accept the faith of Chalcedon and followed the
monophysite doctrine: that Christ had only one nature. The
Patriarch of Constantinople suggested a theological
compromise, which came to be known as monothelitism:
that Christ had two natures but one will. Pope Honorius I
(625-38), anxious to promote unity, approved of the
teaching and Emperor Heraclius issued his *Ekthesis* decree,
making monthelitism the official doctrine of the empire.
However, subsequent theological reflection revealed the
dangers of the doctrine – what sort of a human nature did
Christ have if he lacked a human will? Monothelitism was
condemned by a synod at the Lateran in 649, although this
bold action led to the arrest of St Martin I (649-53) and his
exile to the Crimea. Although Honorius' letters to the
Patriarch could be understood in an orthodox sense, St Leo

II (682-83) eventually condemned his predecessor for his negligence in 'permitting the immaculate faith to be stained'. If Honorius was not a formal heretic, as many opponents of Catholicism have claimed, he was certainly naïve and imprudent.

Soon a new theological controversy served to further increase the distance between Pope and Emperor. In the 720s the doctrine began to spread that it was wrong to make artistic representations of Christ, which culminated in the removal of a prominent image of Christ from the imperial palace. This iconoclastic heresy was quickly condemned by St Gregory II (715-31), despite Emperor Leo III threatening him with deposition should he refuse to approve of the teaching. When his successor, St Gregory III (731-41), proved equally firm, the Emperor confiscated the papal estates in Sicily and southern Italy (which brought in vital revenues) and withdrew from papal jurisdiction a number of important Greek-speaking archbishoprics.

The Carolingians

The papacy had long relied on imperial support against the Lombards, who controlled much of the Italian peninsula. The popes managed to deal with them through bribery and short-lived alliances. There could be gains: in 728, for example, the Lombard King Liutprand entered into an agreement with St Gregory II, handing over Sutri and several hill towns in Latium 'as a gift to the blessed Apostles Peter and Paul'. There were darker periods, such as the siege of Rome under the same Liutprand.

In desperate need of allies, the popes began to look westwards. In 739 St Gregory III (731-41) approached the Franks under Charles Martel for military assistance. There was no response but Martel's son, Pepin III ('the Short'), was more forthcoming. Stephen II (752-57) met Pepin at Ponthion in January 754. During a further meeting at Quierzy, Pepin offered to protect the Roman church and the pope, promising him extensive territories currently held by the Lombards and belonging rightfully to Peter. This was the so-called 'Donation of Pepin', effectively constituting the beginnings of the Papal States, and backed up by the forged 'Donation of Constantine', in which the first Christian Emperor was shown to confer on Silvester I (314-35) dominion over Rome, Italy and 'the provinces, places and *civitates* of the western regions'. The forgery was produced, in the words of one modern historian, 'to give tangible verification of what contemporaries believed was anyway true; it illustrated and authenticated gifts of land that had left no other record for later societies which had come to expect them'.[2]

---

[2] Edward Norman, *The Roman Catholic Church: An illustrated History* (2007), 29

The Pope, in return, anointed Pepin and his family at St
Denis, just outside Paris, and gave him the prestigious title
'patrician of the Romans'. In 755 Pepin invaded Italy,
defeated the Lombards and made his 'donation' a reality.
Although Byzantium remained a powerful force that could
not be ignored, a new period of papal history began, closely
connected to the Frankish monarchy.

Pepin's son, Charlemagne, managed to restore a unity
unseen in western Europe since the Roman Empire and,
after the Lombards besieged Rome once again in 773, he
marched into Italy, occupying Pavia (the Lombard capital)
and declaring himself 'King of the Lombards'.
Charlemagne reconfirmed the 'Donation of Pepin' while
staying in Rome with Hadrian I (772-95) at Easter 774. On
Christmas Day 800 Leo III (795-816) crowned
Charlemagne Roman emperor in St Peter's, cementing the
alliance in which Pope and Frankish emperor would work
together for the glory of God. Rome would claim that
Charlemagne (and his successors) had been anointed to
protect the Church under the supervision of the pontiff,
who had conferred the imperial title. The emperor, on the
other hand, saw himself as gaining his authority from God,
though working with the Church. With hindsight, the idea
of using an empire to further papal prestige and authority
was highly dubious for, in the words of R. W. Southern, 'in
creating an emperor the pope created not a deputy, but a

rival or even a master. The theoretical supremacy implied in the act of creation could never be translated into practical obedience to orders given and received. Hence the pope's practical supremacy over his emperor came to an end at the moment of coronation'. This would dominate papal history for the next millennium.[3]

Charlemagne's long reign is often described as a 'renaissance', during which Christian orthodoxy was defended, scholarship promoted and education encouraged. Monastic houses were reformed and put under the Benedictine Rule, while the Sacred Liturgy and organisation of the Church became more ordered. However, this 'golden age' was not to last for long. Charlemagne's lands were eventually divided between his grandsons and the nobility reasserted their power in matters of both religion and state. Gradually even the imperial title itself fell into disuse.

The ninth century saw the arrival of the Saracens on the pope's doorstep. Sicily became a Muslim colony in the 820s and in August 846 the Arabs attacked Rome itself. The two basilicas outside the city walls, St Peter's and St Paul's, were both badly damaged and desecrated. This led St Leo IV (847-55) to extend the city walls to include St Peter's, creating the so-called 'Leonine city',

---

[3] R. W. Southern, *Western Society and the Church in the Middle Ages* (1970), 99

and to gather together a fleet to defeat the Muslims in a naval battle at Ostia (849).

Another strong leader was St Nicholas 'the Great' (858-67) who, according to a contemporary writer, 'gave orders to kings and rulers as though he were lord of the world' and brought upstart bishops under his control. He refused to recognise the second marriage of King Lothair II of Lorraine and excommunicated the archbishops of Cologne and Trier who had sanctioned the divorce. The dispute even led the Emperor Louis II, Lothair's brother, to lay siege to Rome in 864, though papal authority triumphed in the end. Nicholas likewise excommunicated the new Patriarch of Constantinople, Photius, who had been appointed uncanonically, and ordered the Byzantine Emperor not to interfere in Church affairs: 'the privileges of the Roman church came from the mouth of Christ, who conferred them on Blessed Peter. They can in no way be diminished, infringed upon or changed, because what God has established man cannot change'. There were other disagreements, notably over the Christians in Bulgaria, and a synod held in Constantinople in 867 actually excommunicated and deposed Pope Nicholas. The stage was set for the schism that divided East and West less than two centuries later.

The Medieval Papacy

The 'Bad Popes'

Following the death of St Nicholas the Great, the papacy entered a period of decline and corruption. With the establishment of the Papal States, the pope had to constantly struggle with the local aristocracy and, following the break-up of the Carolingian Empire, the pope became little more than a puppet of the great families – the Theophylacts, the Crescentii, the Tusculani. Many of the popes of the period met violent and suspicious deaths: John VIII (872-82) was first poisoned by his entourage and then beaten to death, while Leo V (903) and the anti-pope Christopher (903-04) were murdered together by order of Sergius III (904-11). Similarly John X (914-28) was suffocated with a pillow and Stephen VIII (939-42) brutally mutilated. Pope Formosus (891-96) managed to die naturally but nine months later his body was exhumed and put on trial in the Lateran, dressed in full pontificals. Accused of perjury and violating the laws forbidding the translation of bishops, the fingers he used for blessing were hacked off and his corpse thrown into the Tiber. Formosus' real crime, though, was that he had sided with the wrong faction to that of the current pope, Stephen VI (896-97), who himself was strangled shortly after the 'cadaver synod'.

Cardinal Baronius, one of the first modern papal historians, famously described the papacy during the period as a 'pornocracy' – rule by harlots. Here he was thinking of several strong women from the Theophylact dynasty, namely Theodora and her daughter Marozia, who exercised great control in Rome. The latter not only engineered the elections of John X, Leo VI (928) and Stephen VII (928-31) but was the lover of Sergius III, by whom she bore a son, the future John XI (931-36). Marozia also counted a pope among her grandchildren: John XII (955-64). He became pope as a teenager and led a decadent lifestyle, turning the Lateran into a den of iniquity. Despite his obvious shortcomings, John was not shy in asserting papal primacy and in 960 offered the imperial crown to Otto I, King of Germany, in return for his help. Otto confirmed the donations of Pepin and Charlemagne and was duly crowned and anointed in St Peter's on 2 February 962; the Holy Roman Empire was back and would remain a fixture until the age of Napoleon. Using his new authority, Otto insisted that newly-elected popes needed imperial approval and then tried to depose John because of his scandalous conduct.

The pope refused to relent and fled to the country when Ottonian troops entered Rome. He died not on the battlefield but, if tradition is to be believed, while in bed with a married woman.

Powerful matrons like Theodora and Marozia probably contributed to the myth of Pope Joan, the story that a woman (some say from England) disguised herself as a man and worked her way up the Roman curia, eventually being elected pope. Her daring scheme was only discovered when she became pregnant and gave birth during a papal procession. The legend was widely believed and her bust was even included with those of other popes in Siena Cathedral until 1601. However the earliest surviving source dates from the twelfth century and the 'popess' appears in no creditable lists of pontiffs. Even her supposed dates vary from one source to another.

The 'bad popes' of the period, despite everything, were still regarded as the successors of St Peter, dignified in their office if not their person. They held fast to the deposit of faith and asserted the Roman primacy. Even the scandalous John XII had an interest in monastic reform and gave the pallium to a great pastor like St Dunstan of Canterbury (960). John XV (985-96) may have been deeply unpopular in Rome but became the first pope to solemnly canonize a saint, Ulrich of Augsburg, in 993 – an important step for the papacy.

Gregorian Reform

As the second millennium dawned, the papacy was still very much the plaything of the leading Roman families. Three popes from the Tusculani family, based near Frascati, sat on the fisherman's throne: Benedict VIII (1012-24), John XIX (1024-32) and Benedict IX (1032-44, 1045, 1047-48), the latter being unique in having three different spells as pope. Being deposed for the final time in 1048, he turned his back on a dissolute life and ended his days at the monastery of Grottaferrata.

At the same time, there was a growing movement for church reform, centred on great monastic houses such as Cluny in France and Gorze in Germany. The King of Germany, Henry III, was personally devout and convinced of the need for reform in head and members. When he travelled to the Eternal City for imperial coronation in 1046 he put his ideal into reality by convoking councils at Sutri and Rome. Finding three claimants to the papal throne, Henry selected his former court chaplain, Suidger of Bamberg, who became Clement II (1046-47). Several other German popes followed who took reform seriously, the greatest (and longest-lived) of whom was St Leo IX (1049-54). Soon after election he convened a synod at Rome that condemned simony and clerical concubinage. He travelled around Europe taking the message of reform with him ; the first year of the pontificate saw him at

Pavia, Rheims and Mainz. However his image as an other-worldly reformer was compromised in 1054 when he led an army against the Normans in southern Italy and was himself captured in battle. The papal invasion had also entered territory over which Constantinople claimed jurisdiction. It proved to be the final straw in the on-going tensions. Leo sent a delegation to the Byzantine Emperor but both sides refused to compromise and pope and patriarch ended up excommunicating each other in July 1054. This is widely considered as the moment when schism split East from West.

One of St Leo's inner circle was Hildebrand, a Cluniac monk who was later himself elected as St Gregory VII (1073-85). As well as attempting to counter simony and clerical marriage, St Gregory attacked lay investiture, the appointment to ecclesiastical offices by laymen and their conferring of the insignia of office, such as the episcopal crozier and ring. St Gregory had a high ideal of the pope, believing that all the faithful, including emperors and kings, owed him loyalty and obedience, and formulated these claims in a series of twenty-seven propositions known as the *Dictatus Papae* of 1075: 'the pope can be judged by no-one', 'the Roman church has never erred,' 'the pope alone can depose and restore bishops', 'all princes should kiss his feet', even 'he can depose emperors'.

The papacy still had many weak spots, as was demonstrated following the death of Honorius II (1124-30) when tensions between the Pierleone and Frangipani families led to the election of two rival candidates: Innocent II (1130-43) and Anacletus II (1130-38). However, the legacy of St Gregory VII continued and the papacy grew in confidence. This was dramatically shown at the Council of Clermont in 1096 when Blessed Urban II called the 'First Crusade', uniting much of Christendom in an effort to protect the Holy Land and establishing a Latin Kingdom of Jerusalem (1099-1291). Moreover, a bureaucracy developed at the papal court and ancient roles such as the College of Cardinals were reorganised. Nicholas II (1059-61) decreed that the cardinals should henceforth elect the new pontiff. Until then popes had usually been selected by the neighbouring bishops and Roman clergy. The scattered ecclesiastical laws began to be codified, especially through the jurist Gratian's massive D*ecretum* (c.1140), and general councils were held at the Lateran in 1123, 1139 and 1179. Historians have spoken of the emergence of a 'papal monarchy' and the trappings of power borrowed elements from the classical and Byzantine past. Papal thrones, like that at Santa Maria in Cosmedin, used the best materials and featured lion arm-rests. Innocent II was even buried in a porphyry coffin thought to have been that of the Emperor Hadrian.

The mid twelfth century saw the reign of the first and so far only English pope, Adrian IV (1154-59). Born at Abbot's Langley in Hertfordshire, Nicholas Breakspear studied in France, joined the canons regular of Saint Ruf at Avignon and never set foot in England as an adult. Appointed Cardinal Bishop of Albano in 1149, he led a highly successful mission as papal legate to Scandinavia, where he brought order to the Church and established Trondheim as the metropolitan see of Norway. As pope, Adrian IV had to defend his position against a hostile Roman commune and a determined German king, Frederick Barbarossa, who was crowned emperor on 18 June 1155. He seems to have been the first to use the title 'Vicar of Christ', stressing the pope's supreme and universal primacy of honour and jurisdiction, founded on Christ.

The Age of Innocent III

The high point of the medieval papacy was undoubtedly the reign of Innocent III (1198-1216). A Roman nobleman and lawyer, he was only thirty-eight at his election and had been made a cardinal by his uncle, Clement III (1187-91). Trained in law, he combined genuine piety and zeal with a sharp intellect and understanding of human affairs. Innocent not only claimed supreme spiritual and temporal authority, like most medieval popes, but actually exercised it.

First he established his authority over the troublesome Roman nobility and won back control of the Papal States. Innocent then looked further afield. In Germany he intervened in the succession crisis following the death of Henry VI, favouring Otto of Brunswick and stressing that the pope alone could grant the imperial crown. Otto IV was eventually crowned in 1209, though he was censured after invading southern Italy. In England he excommunicated King John in 1209 after refusing to recognise Stephen Langton as Archbishop of Canterbury (a papal appointment). For four years England was under interdict. John eventually submitted and made his domains a papal fief, hoping for the pope's support against the French. Innocent mounted the 'Fourth Crusade', although this was disastrously diverted to Constantinople due to the machinations of Venice. Innocent put a brave face on the Fall of Constantinople, hoping that the newly-established Latin Patriarchate would strengthen the unity of the Church.

Innocent was also concerned for the state of the Church and promoted reform movements, famously encouraging St Francis of Assisi and authorising the first Franciscans to preach the Gospel. At the end of his life Innocent called the Fourth Lateran Council (1215), making many important pronouncements still in effect today – such as the doctrine of transubstantiation and the

requirement to go to confession and communion at least
once a year.

The dominant force in European politics in the early
thirteenth century was Frederick II, 'the Wonder of the
World', whose coronation as emperor was sanctioned by
Innocent III in 1215 and took place five years later. His
aim of uniting the Empire with the Kingdom of Sicily,
which he had inherited from his mother, led to frequent
conflicts with Rome and several excommunications.
Gregory IX (1227-41) raised an army of mercenaries to
attack the Emperor and set up a rival King in Germany.
Although a truce was arranged that lasted nine years, by
the end of the pontificate the emperor was calling for a
general council to judge the pope and encircled Rome
with his army. Frederick found his fiercest foe in Innocent
IV (1243-54). At the First Council of Lyons (1245) the
emperor was deposed and the German princes invited to
elect a new king. Innocent eventually managed to claim
Sicily for the Papal States, after Frederick's death, and set
up court in Naples. It fell to Urban IV (1261-64) to offer
the Sicilian crown to Charles of Anjou, brother of St
Louis IX of France, in return for money, military aid and
freedom for the Church in the kingdom.

The popes may have thought they had finally
triumphed over the Hohenstaufen dynasty but the new
King of Sicily proved to be equally problematic. Using

divisions within the College of Cardinals and the Roman nobility to his advantage, Charles managed to make his presence felt. There were a series of short pontificates and long conclaves. It took three years to choose Blessed Gregory X (1271-76) and it might have taken longer had the people of Viterbo not locked the cardinals into the palace and threatened to cut off their supply of food. In 1274 Gregory issued a constitution outlining the procedures relating to papal elections, stressing that the cardinals should meet not more than ten days after the pope's death and stay together until a successor was chosen, without access to the outside world. The modern conclave was born.

Yet, despite this new protocol, there was a two year vacancy following the death of Nicholas IV (1288-92). One day the deadlocked cardinals received a letter from an eremitical abbot and founder of the Celestine Order, encouraging them to quickly elect a pope so as to avoid the wrath of God. The cardinals decided to elect this octogenarian holy man, who became St Celestine V (1294), the 'angelic pope'. Close to God he may have been but he was no administrator or diplomat and the pope became little more than the puppet of the King of Naples, who had supported the Celestine Order in the past. After six months St Celestine resigned, the first pope to do so, but rather than retiring into solitude was kept under house arrest until his death in 1296. 'I wanted nothing in this world but a cell', he would say, 'and a cell they have given me'. He probably died naturally, although a nail-shaped hole in his skull has led to suggestions that he was murdered.

Exile and the Great Schism

The Papacy at Avignon (1309-78)

The 'angelic pope' was succeeded by the more astute and ambitious Boniface VIII (1294-1303). He can be credited for reorganising the Vatican archives and library, establishing a university at Rome and calling the first 'Holy Year' in 1300, attracting tens of thousands of pilgrims to the Eternal City and increasing the prestige of the papacy. Boniface condemned the French king, Philip the Fair, for taxing the clergy in order to pay for his war against England. In 1302 he issued the bull *Unam sanctam* which spoke of two swords, the spiritual and the temporal. 'The first is wielded by the Church; the second is wielded on behalf of the church. The first is wielded by the hands of the priest, the second by the hands of kings and soldiers, but at the wish and by the permission of the priests'. Philip responded by accusing the pope, amongst other things, of immorality and heresy. Boniface was kidnapped by the French at Anagni, where he was preparing a bull of excommunication. Although he was rescued, the traumatized pope died soon afterwards.

The 'outrage of Anagni' had an important consequence. Boniface's successor, Blessed Benedict XI

(1303-04), only survived nine months and the resulting conclave lasted nearly a year. Eventually the Archbishop of Bordeaux was elected as Clement V (1305-14) and crowned at Lyons in the presence of King Philip. He stayed in France due to the political turmoil of central Italy and in the hope he could pacify relations between France and England. By 1309 he was at Avignon, a city belonging to the counts of Provence and surrounded by the papally-owned Comtat-Venaissin. Through accident rather than design, Avignon became the headquarters of the papacy between 1309 and 1378, a period often referred to as the Church's 'Babylonian Captivity'. The city had good communication links with the rest of Europe and was far removed from the horrific memories of Anagni. The popes built a fortified palace and used a summer residence at Châteauneuf-du-Pape, now famous as a centre of wine production. Many of the leading cardinals built magnificent residences or livrées across the river from Avignon at Villeneuve.

During the period the papacy unsurprisingly became 'Frenchified'. All the Avignon popes were French and most of the cardinals they created were fellow countrymen. Many of the popes were strong leaders, able to follow their policies without hindrance from the warring Roman families. John XXII (1316-34) introduced important administrative and economic reforms, extending papal appointment of bishops and papal taxation ('annates') across Europe. Clement VI (1342-52) established a spectacular court, surrounding himself with artists and scholars and commenting that 'my predecessors did not know how to be pope'. During the Black Death, however, he showed great charity and courage, providing a cemetery for the burial of victims and welcoming the Jews into the city, who were escaping from the mobs who blamed them for the pestilence.

The pope remained bishop of Rome and successor of St Peter. All the Avignon pontiffs had the intention of returning to the Eternal City when the moment was right. Innocent VI (1352-62) named a Spanish cardinal as legate to Italy to prepare for the pope's return through diplomacy and, if necessary, warfare. Urban V (1362-70) entered Rome in 1367, where he crowned Charles IV as emperor, but returned to Avignon in 1370 owing to political turbulence. Seven years later Gregory XI (1370-78) settled in Rome, this time permanently, partly due to the encouragement of St Catherine of Siena. He died shortly afterwards in 1378.

The Great Schism (1378-1417)

After the death of Gregory XI, the Roman mobs demanded an Italian candidate and the nervous cardinals chose the Archbishop of Bari, who was duly crowned as Urban VI

(1378-89). He was a compromise candidate since he was born in Naples but had links to Avignon, where he had been a central figure in the curia. However, the French cardinals declared his election as invalid, since it had been done under duress. They also questioned Urban's sanity and fitness to rule. An alternative conclave was thus held and the election of the Swiss anti-pope Clement VII (1378-94) at Fondi inaugurated the Great Schism, during which there were two (and at one stage three) claimants to the throne of the fisherman. This state of affairs divided Christendom and weakened the mission of the Church, which increasingly became a pawn of the European powers. England and the Holy Roman Empire supported Pope Urban and his successors, while France, Scotland and Castile pledged loyalty to Clement; St Catherine of Siena was 'Urbanist' while St Vincent Ferrer was 'Clementine'.

Disillusionment led to the growth of the Lollard and Hussite heresies, based in England and Bohemia respectively and rejecting the hierarchical Church. Faced with such disorder, many believed that the best way to solve the Great Schism was to hold a council. Some argued that a general council was 'the supreme tribunal of God on earth', with the power to depose or override an individual pontiff. This theory was known as conciliarism.

In 1408 the cardinals (rather than the pope) called a council at Pisa, which duly deposed the rival claimants

and elected Alexander V (1409-10). However, since the
other two popes refused to submit, this meant that there
were now three pontiffs. A further council was called at
Constance (1414-17) by the German King Sigismund,
who was anxious to unite Christendom against the
Hussite revolutionaries in Bohemia. The council hoped to
restore unity, counter heresy and reform the Church in
head and members. In the first of these aims Constance
was successful - it deposed the antipopes John XXIII
(1410-15) and Benedict XIII (1394-1417), accepted the
abdication of Gregory XII (1406-15) and elected a single
pope, Martin V (1417-31). To justify themselves, the
Fathers taught that the highest authority in the Church
was a general council rather than the pope – an
extraordinary teaching for an extraordinary time. In order
to demonstrate the council's orthodoxy, Jan Hus (the
leader of the Hussite heresy) was tried and burned at the
stake, despite having been given an imperial guarantee of
safety. Attempts at reform were left to various national
concordats, although once the schism was ended there
was a lack of determination to press on with reform. The
decree *Frequens* (1417) stipulated that councils would
meet regularly in the life of the Church.

The Council of Basel (1431-43), summoned by
Martin V but only meeting after his death, tried to keep
the flame of conciliarism alive. The new pope, Eugenius

IV (1431-37), mistrusted the council's agenda and dissolved the gathering at the end of 1431. The council refused to disperse, pointing to the decrees of Constance that placed a general council above the pope. The pope eventually recognised proceedings but transferred the council to Ferrara (1437) and then Florence (1439), where an act of union was briefly effected between the Latin and Eastern Churches. The Greeks needed support against the Turks and recognised the pope's primacy. Prepared statements were drawn up regarding the Trinity, the Eucharist and purgatory. Meanwhile the remnant at Basel deposed Eugenius and elected in his place Duke Amadeus VIII of Savoy, who became the anti-pope Felix V.

Secular princes took the opportunity of the quarrel to claim control of the church in their territories. The Pragmatic Sanction of Bourges was signed with France in 1438, which was the effective beginning of the 'Gallican liberties', (whereby the authority of the monarch preceded that of the pope in local ecclesiastical appointments and decisions), largely maintained up until the French Revolution. It was left to Pius II (1458-64) to condemn the cardinals' teaching that a general council was superior to the pope in the Bull *Execrabilis* (1460).

The Renaissance Popes

In the aftermath of the schism, the popes set about reasserting their authority. One of the ways of doing this and, at the same time, giving glory to God (and their own families) was by great building projects and artistic commissions. This was desperately needed because the fabric of Rome had been neglected during the Avignon Papacy and parts of the city were in a ruinous state.

The Renaissance Popes are often dismissed as being extravagant and immoral. Alexander VI (1492-1503), from the Spanish Borgia family, fathered at least nine illegitimate children and openly kept a mistress even after his election. He shamelessly aggrandised his family, creating duchies for his sons out of papal land and arranging advantageous marriages for his daughter Lucrezia. The Borgia name came to be irretrievably associated with banquets and poison. However, much of this 'black legend' originated with his enemies, particularly Julius II (1503-13). Though his sexual immorality and nepotism cannot be denied, Alexander actually took his stewardship of the Church seriously. He showed an interest in reform, welcomed crowds of pilgrims to Rome for the Holy Year of 1500 and tried to unite Christendom in a crusade against the Turks. The fact that Christendom recognised him as the supreme arbitrator was revealed in 1493, when he drew a line of

demarcation west of the Azores. Everything to the east of
the line belonged to Portugal and everything to the west
was in the hands of Spain. It is because of the Borgia
Pope that Portuguese is spoken in Brazil and Spanish in
the rest of Latin America.

Julius II was just as likely to be seen leading his army
in armour as leading a service in pontifical robes and was
known as *il terribile* because of his fierce character. Yet
he strengthened the Papal States and left it effectively
unchallenged until the nineteenth century. This was the
age of the 'Italian Wars', when the great powers of
Europe fought over the peninsula, and so resentful was
Louis XII towards the pope's anti-French policies that a
council was called at Pisa to try to depose him. This was
supported by the Holy Roman Emperor, Maximilian I,
who himself had designs on the papacy. Julius reacted by
calling a council himself in 1512 (Lateran V) and
narrowly escaped the crisis. Julius reformed religious
orders, attacked simony and established the first
bishoprics in South America. He was a great patron of the
arts, asking Bramante to design a new basilica of St Peter,
Raphael to decorate the papal apartments (with
masterpieces such as *The School of Athens*) and
Michelangelo to paint the ceiling of the Sistine Chapel.
He also set up a permanent 'regiment' of mercenaries
from the cantons of Lucerne and Zurich and apparently

asked Michelangelo to design the uniform of these 'Swiss Guards'. Every visitor to Rome can be thankful for the legacy of this 'warrior pope'.

Julius' successor was Leo X (1513-21), aged only thirty-seven, who famously said on his election: 'now that God has given us the papacy, let us enjoy it'. This did not prevent him from getting on with serious work. He concluded the Fifth Lateran Council and set up commissions to look at church reform. Leo also negotiated the Concordat of Bologna with France (1516). In return for recognition of papal prerogatives and the payment of annates, the French King was given the right to appoint bishops and other prelates. After decades of raising the spectre of conciliarism, France recognised the abolition of the Pragmatic Sanction.

Leo continued the work of rebuilding St Peter's and sanctioned an Indulgence that would increase funds for this ambitious project. A German Augustinian, Martin Luther, saw this as riddled with corruption and went on to attack many other Catholic teachings and practices. His ideas spread quickly and were encouraged by many German princes, who recognised in the crisis an opportunity to extend their power. Leo eventually condemned Luther in *Exsurge Domine* (1520) and excommunicated him. When Henry VIII wrote an anti-Lutheran treatise in defence of the sacraments, Leo honoured the English King with the title 'Defender of the Faith', which can still be found on British coinage.

Rome was slow to react to the Protestant Reformation and both Leo X and his Dutch-born successor, Hadrian VI (1522-23), appeared more concerned with the need to mount a crusade against the Turks, who had recently taken Belgrade and Rhodes. Clement VII (1523-34) was a weak leader, whose disastrous foreign policy led to the Emperor Charles V invading the Papal States, sacking Rome (6 May 1527) and taking the pope prisoner for six months. During these hostilities 147 Swiss Guards were killed.

Clement had to deal with Henry VIII over his marital difficulties. The Holy See was used to problems arising from royal marriages – indeed, Julius II had granted Henry a dispensation so that he could marry Catherine of Aragon, his late brother's widow, in the first place. However, this new case proved to be a difficult one: not only was theological opinion on the Queen's side but the Pope knew himself to be at the mercy of Catherine's nephew, the Emperor. Clement procrastinated and delayed his final decision, but ultimately did not compromise in defending the marriage bond. The stalemate ended dramatically in 1533 when Henry VIII broke with Rome and declared himself head of the new

Church of England, Clement in the meantime excommunicating the English King.

Clement eventually made an uneasy peace with Charles V and crowned him as Holy Roman Emperor in Bologna in 1530, the last time a pope would preside at such an event. Clement also promised to call a general council, which the Emperor saw as the only possible solution to the Protestant schism, although this never materialized and was left to his successor, Paul III (1534-49).

Reformation and Revolution

The Catholic Reformation

Calls for reform in the Church were not only found in Protestant circles but also within the Church, as seen in the emergence of new 'reformed' orders such as the Oratory of Divine Love (1497), Theatines (1524), Barnabites (1530) and Jesuits (1540). The latter have a special place in the history of the Church for their commitment to promoting reform, providing education in the Faith, encouraging a love for the Church (including the pope) and taking the Gospel to all corners of the world. Reform was also suggested by local synods and initiatives such as the commission of cardinals, including Reginald Pole, which produced the *Consilium de emendanda Ecclesia* in 1537.

The crucial impetus for a Catholic revival was the Council of Trent, called by Paul III in 1542 and meeting in three sessions between 1545 and 1563. Despite the long-drawn nature of the Council, due to political factors, Trent reaffirmed the Catholic Faith, refuted Protestant beliefs and underlined the Church's tradition. The Church was comprehensively reformed – seminaries would be created for priestly formation, bishops were ordered to be resident in their dioceses, preaching and catechesis were encouraged and new editions of liturgical books published.

The great task of the papacy was now to apply the decrees of Trent. Perhaps the most famous of the 'Tridentine' popes was St Pius V (1566-72), a Dominican whose mendicant habit led to all subsequent popes wearing a white cassock. He avoided nepotism, scaled down the papal court and published the Roman Catechism (1566), the revised Roman breviary (1568) and Roman Missal (1570). A former inquisitor, he supported the work of the Roman Inquisition in countering heresy and established the Index (1571) to condemn erroneous books. His political interventions were not always successful – his excommunication of Elizabeth I (1570) had little effect and made matters worse for her Catholic subjects – but St Pius managed to form a Holy League against the expansionist Turks, who were defeated at the naval battle of Lepanto (1571). The pope attributed this to Our Lady and the praying of the rosary and instituted the feast of Our Lady of Victories (7 October).

These policies were continued by St Pius' successor, Gregory XIII (1572-85). Before ordination he had fathered a son and as pope doted over his grandchildren.

However, he had had a personal conversion, influenced by St Charles Borromeo, and energetically pursued Tridentine reform. Gregory published a new edition of the Corpus of Canon Law (1582) and opened colleges that aimed to produce well-trained clerics, armed with the latest spiritual and intellectual weapons. In Rome he founded the Greek (1577), Hungarian (1578) and English (1579) Colleges and reconstituted the Roman College (1572). Elsewhere he established a Swiss College in Milan and at Braunsberg and Olmütz institutions to provide missionaries for Protestant Scandinavia. Gregory was a keen supporter of the Jesuits, who directed many of these colleges and sent missions across the known world. Shortly before his death in 1585, Gregory received four ambassadors from the Kings of Bungo, Arima and Omura – all of whom had been converted by Jesuit missionaries working in Japan.

Pope Gregory is best remembered today for his reform of the Julian Calendar, which had been called for by many voices down the centuries. The calendar year, as set by Julius Caesar in 45 B.C., was 11 minutes longer than the solar year, which amounted to an error of a day every 125 years. This was not simply a matter of technical detail for it had consequences relating to the vexed question of the dating of Easter. The 1582 Bull *Inter gravissimas* decreed the removal of ten days to correct the calendar's drift. Protestant Europe ignored this change and Great Britain only adopted the Gregorian calendar in 1752 - making Voltaire comment: 'the English mob preferred their calendar to disagree with the Sun than to agree with the Pope'.

The Age of Absolutism

After the austerity of many of the 'Tridentine' popes, the reign of Urban VIII (1623-44) signified a return to magnificence and spectacle; as one contemporary noted, 'he wished to be seen as a prince rather than as a pope, a ruler rather than as a pastor'. Soon after his election two nephews and a brother-in-law received the red hat, all to the glory of the Barberini family. He also built the massive Palazzo Barberini and commissioned Bernini's famous *baldacchino* (canopy) over the apostle's tomb at St Peter's, decorated with the family arms and swarms of golden Barberini bees. Yet Urban took his spiritual duties seriously – revising the Divine Office, founding the Collegio Urbano to train missionaries, insisting that bishops should reside in their dioceses and approving new religious orders, including the Visitation (1626) and St Vincent de Paul's Lazarists (1632). Posterity remembers him, however, for the condemnation of his scientist friend, Galileo Galilei. In truth, Rome never used the word 'heresy' in connection with Galileo and merely questioned his interpretation of Scripture and his insistence that the earth orbiting the sun was fact and not simply a proposition (and one that was not actually proved until the following century).

Urban's pontificate coincided with the Thirty Years War (1618-48), a conflict as much to do with dynastic rivalries as dealing with the consequences of the Reformation. The pope saw himself as the common father of Christendom and supreme adjudicator between the nations. It was unfortunate, then, that such universal pretentions were marred by his pro-French sympathies. When the Peace of Westphalia finally ended hostilities in 1648 and redrew the confessional map of Europe, no papal representative was invited to join the negotiations. The protests of the then pope Innocent X (1644-55) fell on deaf ears and the papacy would henceforth be excluded from all major international treaties.

The popes also had to contend with 'absolutist' monarchs who were growing in power and self-confidence and who tried to minimise unwanted 'interference' from Rome. In France, for example, there was a tendency towards Gallicanism, finding inspiration in the Pragmatic of Bourges (1438) and stressing independence from Rome and regarding the pope as little more than a figurehead. For Louis XIV the French Church was almost a department of State and the

'Gallican Articles' of 1682 asserted the superior authority of general councils, the age-old privileges of the French Church and denied papal authority over kings or affairs of State. Gallicanism quickly became associated with Jansenism, a Protestantising strain within Catholicism which stressed the sinful condition of mankind. Papal condemnations of the Jansenists, culminating with *Unigenitus* (1713) of Clement XI (1700-21), were seen as attacks on France and nearly led to schism. Gallicanism and Jansenism inspired similar movements across Europe, including Febrionianism in Austria.

During the period the popes moved their court from the Vatican to the Quirinale, on the opposite side of the city. The popes themselves were generally pious and well-intentioned. Blessed Innocent XI (1676-89) stood out for his personal holiness and lack of nepotism. Benedict XIII (1724-30), who had given up a dukedom in order to become a Dominican, lived a monastic lifestyle, visiting hospitals and even catechizing children himself. Unusually, as well as being bishop of Rome he retained the archbishopric of Benevento and took a lively interest in diocesan affairs. The down side of such worthy interests was that he left the business of politics to others, most notably his unscrupulous Secretary of State, Cardinal Niccolò Coscia.

Perhaps the greatest of the eighteenth century popes was Benedict XIV (1740-58). Prior to election he had worked in the curia, publishing an influential work on using 'modern' historical techniques in the processes for beatification and canonization, and served as bishop of his native Bologna. As pope, Benedict brought much intelligence, energy and wit to the office. He liked to walk around Rome in wig and tricorn hat; whereas his predecessors were only seen in public a few times a year, Benedict was just as likely to be found talking to his poorer subjects in the streets as at the Quirinale.

Pope Benedict pursued a reforming agenda, to varying degrees of success. In the Papal States, taxes were reduced and administration streamlined. He condemned the forcible baptism of Jews and ruled that the baptism of the children of Jews or pagans without parental consent was valid but illicit. Benedict signed concordats with Sardinia (1741), Naples (1741), Spain (1753) and Austria (1757) and his friendly relations with the King of Prussia (a Lutheran but with many Catholic subjects) prevented the establishment of a national church, essentially independent of Rome. He wrote to the Portuguese bishops of South America, asking for the better treatment of the Indians.

Above all, Pope Benedict is remembered for his scholarly and antiquarian interests. He made changes in the liturgy, founded four learned Academies in Rome, established the Capitoline Museum and reorganized the Vatican Library. He was admired by many who had otherwise ambivalent attitudes towards his Church, including Voltaire and the Sultan Mahmoud. Despite his tolerant outlook, he was careful to condemn Freemasonry and the more radical writings of the Enlightenment.

Just before his death, Benedict ordered an investigation into the Portuguese Jesuits, who were accused of inappropriate commercial activities. The Jesuits had long been unpopular – the *philosophes* saw them as keeping superstition alive and holding back the 'Enlightenment'; other religious orders and the diocesan clergy saw them as rivals and resented their influence; governments were suspicious of their power. The chief minister in Portugal, the Marquis of Pombal, thought the Society of Jesus obstructed his plans to 'modernise' the Church and even threatened imperial interests with their 'Reductions', self-governing village communities in Paraguay. They were even suspected of an assassination attempt on King Joseph I, resulting in the expulsion of Jesuits in 1759 and the burning at the stake of the octogenarian Father Malagrida two years later.

In France the Jesuits were regarded as the key opponents of Jansenism and Gallicanism and Louis XV eventually suppressed them in the Kingdom in 1764.

Other countries soon followed suit. Pressure was put on the papacy for a universal suppression and the conclave of 1769 was dominated by the issue, Cardinal Ganganelli being elected as Clement XIV (1769-74) chiefly because he had indicated that such drastic action might be possible and advantageous. He procrastinated for several years but finally capitulated to diplomatic pressure and suppressed the Jesuits with the 1773 Brief *Dominus ac Redemptor*. After signing the document, Clement commented: 'I have cut off my right hand". A pope suppressing the body that supported him the most loyally was clear proof of the Church's political weakness.

Revolution

The results of the suppression of the Jesuits were far-reaching: missionary activity was reduced, hundreds of colleges were put in jeopardy and scores of writers and scholars, badly needed in a period of intellectual attack on the Church, were declared suspect. Continued challenges had to be faced by Clement's successor, Pius VI (1775-99). Despite declining papal finances, he lived the life of a Renaissance pontiff: patronizing artists and lavish building projects, taking pride in grandiose spectacles, and enriching his family along the way. However, he was keenly aware of the dangers that faced the Church.

The Holy Roman Emperor, Joseph II (a member of the Habsburg dynasty), had launched on his own programme to rationalise the Church. He was known as 'the sacristan' due to the attention he paid to details of religious observance: he banned many popular pilgrimages and devotions, preferred plain vestments made of leather to those made from ornate fabrics, suppressed a third of all religious houses (mostly contemplative) and visualised parish clergy as glorified civil servants. Pius VI travelled to Vienna to meet the Emperor in 1782 – a rare papal excursion beyond the alps. Despite an enthusiastic welcome from the crowds, he won no concessions from Joseph. Meanwhile the Emperor's brother Leopold, Grand Duke of Tuscany, sponsored a diocesan synod at Pistoia in 1786, which pursued modernising reforms and adopted the anti-papal Gallican Articles of 1682. The pope subsequently condemned the Pistoian reforms in 1794.

By that time, traditional elites across Europe were terrified by the French Revolution, with its bloody campaign against monarchy, nobility and clergy. The Civil Constitution of the Clergy effectively nationalised the Church in 1790 but Pius hesitated before denouncing this as schismatic and suspending all clergy who took an oath of loyalty to the new regime. The French Church became split between the Constitutional Church, now in schism, and the 'refractory priests', who refused the oath and were assumed to be counter-revolutionaries. Many clergy and religious lost their lives in the 'Reign of Terror'. French troops seized the papal possessions of Avignon and Venaissin and eventually invaded Italy. In 1796 Napoleon set up republics in Milan and Venice and then set his sights on freeing 'the Roman people from their long slavery'. The pope felt he had no other option than to negotiate a peace with humiliating concessions. The resulting Peace of Tolentino (1797) involved the disbanding of the papal army (such as it was), the abandonment of claims upon papal territory now in French hands, the handing over of valuable manuscripts and art treasures, and the payment of 30 million lire. Finally on 20 February 1798 the octogenarian pope was forced out of Rome and was taken to various destinations, before settling at the citadel of Valence in Dauphiné. Here he died the following August. Many thought that with him would die the papacy.

Restoration

Pius VI had shown much weakness and indecision in the face of aggressive monarchs and revolutionaries. However, the dignity with which he bore his final exile and imprisonment made many regard him a martyr and thus raised the prestige of the papacy. Moreover, he left instructions for the election of his successor despite the occupation of Rome. The cardinals met under Austrian protection at the monastery of San Giorgio Maggiore in Venice and, after fourteen weeks of deliberations, Cardinal Chiaramonte, a Benedictine and bishop of Imola, became Pius VII (1800-23). Soon after his election he was able to return to Rome.

Aided by a gifted Secretary of State, Cardinal Ercole Consalvi, Pius negotiated a concordat with Napoleon, who was now First Consul and aware of the usefulness of being at good terms with the Church; he thought the pope's authority equivalent to 'a corps of 200,000 men'. An agreement was signed in 1801 and Catholicism in France restored, though it took time to sort out the schism with the Constitutional Church and far-reaching compromises were made – the State had to approve papal documents before they were published in France and even a feast of 'St Napoleon', an obscure and rather dubious martyr, was recognised. In 1805 the pope travelled to Paris for the coronation of Napoleon, although the new Emperor decided to place the crown on his own head once it had been blessed by Pius.

Relations with the Emperor remained tense, especially after the pope refused to back a blockade of England. The French entered Rome in February 1808 and once again the pope was taken prisoner, being confined at Savona, near Genoa, for four years before being transferred to

Fontainebleau. Pius lived the life of a simple Benedictine monk and initially refused to recognise the bishops named by Napoleon. Exhausted and recovering from serious illness, the pope finally bowed to pressure and signed a draft 'Concordat of Fontainebleau' in January 1813. Napoleon envisaged an end to the temporal power of the pope and a permanent move of the papacy to France - a second Babylonian Captivity... While in captivity on St Helena several years later, the former emperor mused: 'I would have exalted the Pope beyond all measure; I would have made him forget the loss of his temporal power. I would have governed the world both of politics and of religion. It would have been a further means of uniting all the federal States of the empire and of maintaining peace. I would have held my religious assemblies side by side with the legislative ones. I would have opened and closed these assemblies, sanctioned and published their canons as did Constantine and Charlemagne'.[4]

The pope was saved only by the failing fortunes of Napoleon, who finally released his prisoner in March 1814. Pius made a triumphant progress back to Rome, entering the city on 24 May, his carriage being drawn through the streets by thirty young men from the most

---

[4] F. Nielson, *The History of the Papacy in XIXth Century* (1906), i.329

notable Roman families. The date was soon declared as
the feast of Our Lady, Help of Christians. His remaining
years were concerned with restorations – of the Papal
States, of the houses and colleges closed by the French,
and of the Jesuits suppressed by his predecessor
Clement XIV.

Pius' immediate successors built on this work of
restoration although they are often unfairly dismissed as
conservative 'reactionaries'. Leo XII (1823-29) was not
so much concerned with politics as with the building up
of the papacy's spiritual and moral authority, even if this
made him unpopular in many quarters. In 1825 he
ignored the advice of his advisers by proclaiming a Holy
Year, which proved to be a great success. Gregory XVI
(1831-46) was a Camaldolese monk, known for his
humour and popular touch, and the last theologian to be
made pope until Benedict XVI. As a young monk he had
written *The Triumph of the Holy See* (1799), an optimistic
title during the period of Pius VI's imprisonment. As
pope, Gregory oversaw the expansion of the Church's
missionary activity and condemned slavery and the slave
trade in 1839. He developed the encyclical letter as a
means of teaching the faithful the truths of the Faith. The
most famous of his letters was *Mirari vos* (1832), which
condemned liberalism and religious indifferentism. In the
political sphere he had to deal with new nations,

including Belgium and the South American republics. The 1831 Bull *Sollicitudo Ecclesiarum* stressed that the Holy See would always deal with *de facto* governments rather than asking complex questions of right and legitimacy. The prestige of the papacy was further enhanced by Ultramontanism, as exemplified by the pro-papalist writings of de Maistre and Chateaubriand, and Romanticism, which looked to the past for inspiration.

Pio Nono

Gregory XVI was succeeded by Blessed Pius IX (1846-78), the longest-reigning pope. Born in 1792, when the French Revolution was at its height, Giovanni Maria Mastai-Ferretti was the ninth child of a minor Roman count. He first considered an army career but was rejected due to his epilepsy – he attributed his eventual cure from this condition to the intercession of Our Lady of Loreto. He was thus able to study for the Priesthood. Ordained in 1819, he worked as director of an orphanage and a hospice and as a diplomat in Chile, before becoming Archbishop of Spoleto and later Imola.

On his election, *Pio Nono* was heralded as a progressive, freeing two thousand political prisoners, involving non-clerics in the government of the Papal States and seeming to favour a united Italy. The great statesman Metternich commented that he had allowed for everything except a liberal pope. However, things were to dramatically change. In 1848 revolution spread through many European countries. In Rome the pope's prime minister, Count Pellegrino Rossi, was assassinated by radicals and Pius was forced to flee to the coastal town of Gaeta, near the Neapolitan border. He appealed to the Catholic world and eventually returned to Rome in 1850, with the help of French troops.

Many saw Pius metamorphose from being a liberal into a 'reactionary' after 1848. In truth, his original intentions had been misunderstood. He increasingly saw himself as engaged in a great battle for the survival of the Faith against the 'tyranny' of liberalism. He saw the new democracies as claiming to control every area of life, abolishing traditional responsibilities and privileges, and threatening the independence of the Church. In 1864, for example, Pius produced the *Syllabus of Errors*, denouncing the 'principal errors of our times'.

At his election the suggestion had been made that the pope could head a newly united Italy. However, Pius spent much of his pontificate battling with the forces of nationalism and defending the Papal States, with the help of his own army, French troops as well as volunteers from many Catholic countries, including the United Kingdom. Pius believed that the pope's temporal sovereignty was essential for the freedom of the papacy. By 1860 the pope had lost all his possessions except Rome and the immediate area nearby. He hung on thanks to the protection of France, but when the Franco-Prussian War was declared in 1870 the pope became increasingly vulnerable and Rome was captured, becoming capital of the new Italy. The King, Vittorio Emmanuele I, moved into the former papal palace of the Quirinale. Meanwhile, Pius became a self-imposed 'prisoner of the Vatican' and forbade Catholics to take part in Italian politics.

Despite losing the Papal States, *Pio Nono* had a huge impact on the Universal Church. He re-established the hierarchies in England and Wales (1850) and the Netherlands (1853), raised the first American to the dignity of cardinal (John McCloskey, Archbishop of New York) and encouraged missionary work. On 8 December 1854 he defined the Immaculate Conception as dogma, having set up a commission of theologians and consulted with the world's bishops. Then in 1869 he called the first general council since Trent and preparatory commissions prepared *schemata* on the nature of Faith and the relationship between Church and State. The Council was left unfinished in 1870, due to the outbreak of the Franco-Prussian War, and its main work was the Constitution *Dei Filius*, dealing with revelation and faith and reason, themes which were under attack in the nineteenth century. The Vatican Council is chiefly remembered for the definition of papal infallibility, which was not originally intended for the council but strongly encouraged by the bishops. One of the leading 'Infallibilists' was Cardinal Manning of Westminster, while the future Cardinal, John Henry Newman (not present at the council) thought it was an inopportune time for a definition. In the final vote only two bishops voted against, including the American Bishop of Little Rock, much to the delight of the media who spoke of the battle between 'Big Rock' and 'Little Rock'. As the pope issued the definition a loud clap of thunder was heard, being variously interpreted as the disapproval of Heaven or the anger of Hell.

Pius has been accused of anti-semitism, especially in the case of Edgardo Levi-Mortara, a Jewish baby who was baptised by his Catholic nurse when he was seriously ill aged 16 months. When the fact of his baptism became known, the pope ordered Edgardo to be raised as a Christian and was taken into care. This is sometimes referred to as a 'kidnapping'. However, it is worth remembering that throughout the process Edgardo kept in touch with his Jewish family, freely chose to study for the Priesthood and eventually gave testimony for the pope's beatification process. Moreover, Pius improved conditions for the Jews in Rome, abolishing the Ghetto, removing its gates and stationing soldiers to protect the inhabitants.

Pius IX regarded the loss of temporal sovereignty as a disaster for the Church. However, with hindsight, it ensured a revival in papal fortunes. What the pope lost in temporal power he gained in spiritual authority. No longer simply an 'Italian prince', he was increasingly regarded as a worldwide leader and Catholics sympathized with the hardships he faced as 'prisoner of the Vatican'. Helped by the expanding media and the growing ease of travel, pilgrims flocked to Rome not only to visit the tombs of the apostles and the famous shrines and churches, but actually to see the pope, the current successor of Peter. Pius was the first pope to hold regular audiences and charmed pilgrims with his piety and joviality.

The Modern Papacy

Into the Twentieth Century

Pius IX's successor was the frail bishop of Perugia, expected to be little more than a stop-gap. However Leo XIII (1878-1903) would turn out to be the third longest-serving pontiff and a remarkable leader. To a large extent he continued the policies of *Pio Nono*, safeguarding the Faith against the errors of the age, but also showed sensitivity towards modern trends. He promoted a revival of the philosophy of St Thomas Aquinas, opened up the Vatican Archives, encouraged science and astronomy and provided guidelines for the study of Scripture. In his famous encyclical *Rerum Novarum* (1891) Leo applied the Church's teaching to modern capitalism, industry and commerce, defending not only private property but the rights of workers and trade unions.

The situation in Italy was distressing, with the passing of anti-clerical laws that confiscated the property of religious orders and limited religious instruction in schools. Leo sought allies elsewhere, making agreements with the German Chancellor Bismarck, who realised that his anti-Catholic campaign (the *Kulturkampf*) was failing, and with the French Republican government. By the time of his death at the age of 94, Leo had won great respect for the papacy despite the loss of the Papal States and his position as a 'prisoner of the Vatican'.

The next pope, St Pius X (1903-14), was the son of a village postman and one of the few popes to have spent a substantial period as parish priest. He aimed to 'restore all things in Christ', with the help of his London-born Secretary of State, Rafael Merry del Val – the first non-Italian to hold this office. The pope's priorities were in the spiritual sphere: encouraging a high standard of liturgy and sacred music, promoting frequent communion and the religious life of the laity. He was careful to condemn the various theological errors which came under the heading of modernism, issuing the decree *Lamentabili* and the encyclical *Pascendi* (1907). In 1910 he asked parish priests and professors to take an anti-modernist oath and this remained in effect until the 1960s.

His foreign policy insisted on the Church's rights. In France the Napoleonic Concordat was annulled, ecclesiastical property confiscated and the Church officially separated from the State in 1905. St Pius condemned these measures, as he did similar policies in Portugal. He died on 20 August 1914, as World War One was beginning – some say he died of a broken heart.

The pontificate of Benedict XV (1914-22) was dominated by the war and its aftermath. He ensured the Church's neutrality so that he could negotiate and pray for peace and help the victims of war. He opened an office at the Vatican to help repatriate prisoners of war. However, the pope pleased no one and each side accused him of favouring the enemy. The Germans called him 'Maledetto XV', while the allies thought he was pro-German since the Kaiser had seemingly promised the return of the Papal States in the event of a victory. Nevertheless Benedict courageously presented a seven point peace plan based on natural justice rather than military might.

The Battle with New Ideologies

The pope of the inter-war years was Pius XI (1922-39). He was an unusual papal candidate, having spent much of his life in the scholarly surroundings of the Ambrosian and Vatican Libraries and enjoyed mountaineering in his spare time – his one published book was *Climbs on Alpine Peaks*. It was only in 1918 that he was sent on a diplomatic mission to Poland and the year before his election became Archbishop of Milan and cardinal. His first act as pope was to give the *Urbi et Orbi* blessing not from the internal loggia at St Peter's, like his three predecessors, but from the external loggia, facing the city and the world. Seven years later he negotiated the Lateran Treaty with Italy (11 February 1929), creating the Vatican City as an independent, neutral sovereign state. The pope was no longer the 'prisoner of the Vatican' and the 'Roman Question' was, for the time being, solved.

Pius issued a number of important encyclicals, including *Casti connubii* (1930), praising Christian marriage and condemning artificial contraception, and *Quadragesimo anno* (1931), continuing Leo XIII's concern with social teaching. In 1925 he introduced the Feast of Christ the King to remind the faithful that the Lord's Kingship extended to every sphere of human life. In his final years Pius was increasingly concerned with the rise of totalitarian regimes. He faced what he called the 'terrible triangle' of anti-Catholic persecution in Spain, Mexico and the Soviet Union. In 1937 he condemned communism in *Divini Redemptoris* and Nazism in *Mit brennender Sorge*. A concordat had earlier been signed with Nazi Germany (1933), guaranteeing the Church's freedom, but Hitler violated it on a number of occasions and displayed increasing hostility to the Church. *Mit brennender Sorge* caused uproar in Germany and was to be followed by a further document, *Humani Generis Unitas*, attacking aggressive racism, colonialism and nationalism in Germany and elsewhere. Pius XI died before he could complete it.

Pius XI was succeeded by his Secretary of State, Eugenio Pacelli, who became Pius XII (1939-58). During his lifetime and in the years immediately following his death, Pius was widely respected as a man of God and a shepherd of souls, producing important encyclicals on the Church as the Mystical Body of Christ (*Mystici corporis Christi*, 1943), the study of Scripture (*Divino afflante Spiritus*, 1943), the Sacred Liturgy (*Mediator Dei*, 1947) and modern theological dangers (*Humani generis*, 1950). He also had a great devotion to Our Lady and in 1950 defined her Assumption as Catholic dogma. Aware of new forms of media, he made extensive use of television and radio. Millions the world over felt that they knew the 'Angelic Pastor' personally, avidly reading descriptions of his daily routine, his pet goldfinch Gretel and his omnipresent housekeeper, Sr Pasqualina.

In recent years there has been a whole stream of books attacking Pius XII for his 'silence' in the face of the Holocaust. Pius was a highly experienced diplomat who realised the nature of international politics and the delicate position of the Church. In wartime his policy was built, like Benedict XV, around the neutrality of the Church – the Church did not take sides so that it had the freedom to campaign for peace and help all the victims of war.

Modern commentators claim that the Pope could have done more. On paper, to those unaware of the actual historical circumstances, Pius XII could have taken a more open and aggressive policy by clearly condemning the Nazis and denouncing the extermination of the Jews. However, the real question is how effective this would have been. Such was the anti-Catholicism of the Nazi regime that it is unlikely the Pope's words would have changed their policy for the better. The Nazis would certainly have prevented his message from reaching German Catholics. Furthermore, Pius knew very well that a more vocal approach would have made things worse for both the Catholic and Jewish communities. In July 1942 the archbishop of Utrecht issued a Pastoral Letter strongly protesting against the Jewish persecutions in Holland. Immediately, in retaliation, the Nazis rounded up Jews and Catholic non-Aryans and deported them to death camps, including St Edith Stein. Fears of reprisals, not against himself but against the Jews, dominated Pius' thinking. As one historian puts it, 'the very evil to be condemned was sufficiently evil to be able to prevent its condemnation'.[5] Pius suffered greatly, not only for the sufferings of those being killed, but at his own self-imposed silence.

---

[5] J. Derek Holmes. *The Papacy in the Modern World* (1981), p. 168

Behind the scenes, he did as much as possible to support the victims of Nazism. He worked through the Papal Nuncios and other well-disposed contacts in the different occupied countries, to provide shelter, escape routes, money, and documents for the persecuted Jews. It has been reliably calculated that between 600,000 and 850,000 European Jews owed their lives to this hidden work of Catholics with the support of the Pope. In Rome, 155 convents and monasteries sheltered some 5,000 Jews. No less than 3,000 Jews found refuge at the papal summer residence at Castel Gandolfo and Pius himself granted sanctuary within the walls of the Vatican in Rome to hundreds of homeless Jews. Following the Pope's direct instructions, individual Italian priests and monks, cardinals and bishops, were instrumental in saving hundreds of Jewish lives. Overall, while 80% of European Jews perished during World War Two, around 80% of Italy's Jews survived. The Pope also spoke out against the Nazi regime in his Christmas message of 1941, leading the *New York Times* to refer to Pius as 'the only ruler left on the Continent of Europe who dares to raise his voice at all'. The following year he expressed his concern for 'those hundreds of thousands who, without any fault of their own, sometimes only by reason of their nationality or race, are marked down for death or progressive extinction.' Leading Nazis felt that the Pope had abandoned his neutrality, and by July 1943 Hitler was openly discussing his capture. Pius XII's concern for the Jews impressed many outside the Church. In 1945 the Chief Rabbi of Rome, Israel Zolli, became a Catholic and took as his baptismal name 'Eugenio,' in tribute to the pope.

The Second Vatican Council

Pius was succeeded by Cardinal Angelo Roncalli, the seventy-six year-old Patriarch of Venice. Although a short and nondescript pontificate was widely expected, the new pope indicated that things would be different when he chose the name John, the first pope of that name since the middle ages. Blessed John XXIII (1958-63) had other surprises up his sleeve. On 25 January 1959 he announced to the cardinals at St Paul Outside the Walls that he intended to revise canon law, call a synod in Rome and, most ambitiously, convene a general council. There had been talk about a council under Pius XII; the First Vatican Council had, after all, been left unfinished due to political factors. Unlike the other church councils, Pope John's Council was called not to deal with heresy or schism but rather to renew the Church, spread the Gospel and dialogue with the modern world and other Christians. It was primarily a 'pastoral' council.

The synod met at the Lateran in January 1960 and was designed to prepare the way for the Council. Interestingly, it reaffirmed traditional discipline and, among other things, asked for the republication of the Tridentine Catechism. Shortly afterwards preparatory commissions and secretariats were set up and the Second Vatican Council opened amid great splendour on 11 October 1962. It was an unprecedented meeting of the world's Catholic bishops and, included among them, were official observers from other Christian denominations. Prominent among the bishops were those from Rhineland countries who had formulated a plan for *aggiornamento* ('bringing up to date'), with the help of *periti* ('experts') such as Hans Küng, Edward Schillebeeckx, Karl Rahner, Yves Congar and Joseph Ratzinger. This 'Rhine group' eventually came to be opposed by the *Coetus Internationalis Patrum* (International Group of Fathers), including Archbishop Marcel Lefebvre, who went on to establish the traditionalist Society of Pius X and later incurred excommunication for his unauthorised consecration of four bishops. The media encouraged the view that the Council was a battle between conservatives and liberals.

By this time John was suffering from terminal stomach cancer and he watched the sessions on a closed-circuit television in his apartment. He closed the First Session on 8 December 1962 and died before it resumed, mourned by millions around the world. His successor, Paul VI (1963-78), concluded the Council and presided over the application of its teachings. These included a complete revision of the Church's liturgical books, causing both great excitement and disillusionment.

Pope John spoke of the Council as opening the windows of the Church. Much wholesome air came in, as enshrined in the documents *Dei Verbum* (on revelation), *Lumen Gentium* (on the Church), *Sacrosanctum Concilium* (on the Sacred Liturgy) and *Gaudium et Spes* (on the Church in the modern world). However, a fair amount of stormy weather was also let in, especially since the conciliar period coincided with a revolt against tradition in all walks of life and the 'sexual revolution'.

Paul VI was a shy and deeply sensitive man, aware of the loneliness of his office and often taking criticism personally. In 1968 he issued *Humanae Vitae*, reaffirming the Church's condemnation of artificial birth control. Many felt betrayed, especially since a papal commission established to address the subject seemed to point to a different conclusion. The pope never doubted the necessity of the teaching and his four predictions about the consequences of ignoring Church teaching in this area have subsequently been proven to be prophetic. Yet he agonized over the resulting controversy and never wrote another encyclical. The last decade of Paul's pontificate was overshadowed by a depressive pessimism and a personal realisation that, in some areas, 'the smoke of Satan had entered the Church'.

Yet Paul VI became the first 'pilgrim pope' of the modern age. In January 1964, after the finish of the Second Session, he made a pilgrimage to the Holy Land and met the Ecumenical Patriarch in Jerusalem. Further trips followed to Bombay (1964), New York (to speak to the United Nations, 1965), Istanbul (1967), Fatima (1967), Bogota (1968), Geneva (1969), Uganda (1969), the Philippines and Australia (1970). On the last trip he narrowly escaped an assassination attempt in Manila. In this age of easy global travel, pilgrims no longer had to go to Rome to see the pope; the successor of St Peter came to them.

The conclave that met after Paul's death in August 1978 elected a pope in the likeness of 'Good Pope John' – simple, jovial, of peasant stock and formerly Patriarch of Venice. Cardinal Hume famously referred to John Paul I (1978) as 'God's candidate' and yet, only 33 days after his election, he was found dead in his bed. Although many conspiracy theories have tried to explain his sudden demise, it was probably due to his not taking the correct medication for a heart condition.

'God's candidate' was replaced by 'a man from afar': John Paul II (1978-2005), the first non-Italian pope since the Dutch Adrian VI (1522-23). An able philosopher, poet, actor, playwright and sportsman, Karol Wojtyla was a man of great charisma and energy. Like Paul VI, he saw the Church as global, canonising saints from every continent, internationalizing the College of Cardinals and making 104 foreign trips to places as far a field as Guinea-Bissau and the Solomon Islands. Of particular importance was his visit to his native Poland in 1979, allowing him to encourage the Polish people in their struggle with Communism and leading to the Solidarity Movement. Greater visibility meant vulnerability and on 13 May 1981 he was hit by four bullets during a General Audience in St Peter's Square. He attributed his survival to the intercession of Our Lady of Fatima and later met his would-be assassin, Mehmet Ali A ca, in prison.

John Paul reached out to other religions, becoming the first pope since St Peter to enter a synagogue (1986) and also a mosque (2001). He put much emphasis on the pope as teacher and wrote a series of encyclicals and apostolic letters addressing key subjects: Jesus Christ (*Redemptor Hominis*, 1979), Our Lady (*Redemptoris Mater*, 1987), human suffering (*Salvifici Doloris*, 1984), the family (*Familiaris Consortio*, 1981), morality and ethics (*Veritatis Splendor*, 1993), the dignity of human life (*Evangelium Vitae*, 1995) and the relationship between faith and reason (*Fides et Ratio*, 1998). A former professor, he had a special love for young people and presided over ten World Youth Days in various locations between 1984 and 2002, during which the chant could often be heard: 'John Paul 2, we love you'. His death in April 2005 showed that the papacy could still be major news in the twenty-first century. All eyes were turned to Rome and in the United Kingdom the pope's funeral led to the postponement of the Grand National race and a royal wedding.

The German Joseph Ratzinger was elected Benedict XVI (2005-) on 19 April 2005, the feast of the greatest German pope, St Leo IX. Benedict has continued John Paul's vision of the pope as teacher and global pilgrim. The first pope theologian since Gregory XVI, he produced a book, *Jesus of Nazareth* (2007), which was 'in no way an exercise of the magisterium, but is solely an expression of my personal search "for the face of the Lord"'. His encyclicals have dealt with the theological virtues and his teachings have battled with the 'dictatorship of relativism' and stressed the 'hermeneutic of continuity', that the Second Vatican Council did not 're-invent' the Church but should be read in continuity with the Church's tradition. *Summorum Pontificum* (2007) reminded the faithful that the 'extraordinary form' of the Roman Rite, as found in the 1962 Missal of John XXIII, had never been abrogated and remained in the mainstream of modern Catholicism. He has made gestures to strengthen the unity of the Church, particularly with regard to Lefebvrists and traditional or high church Anglicans. In the hope of encouraging dialogue with the Orthodox Churches, he discontinued use of the papal title 'Patriarch of the West'.

Conclusion

The papacy is a remarkable institution, surviving numerous crises down the centuries and adapting itself to new circumstances, while remaining the rock on which Christ built His Church. As the Church expanded and developed, so too did the understanding of the Petrine ministry. The Church did not miraculously appear as a pre-fabricated structure, complete with the Vatican and a well-established hierarchy. The Church grew organically, shaped by events and personalities and led by the Holy Spirit.

The Lord chose Peter as the first pope – the Apostle who walked on water but then began to sink; who made the first profession of faith and moments later blundered into error; who denied his Master three times, despite having sworn he would never do such a thing. Ever since Peter, weak human beings have occupied the Throne of Peter. Some have been saints and born leaders. Many have been weak in their struggles with the political powers or have been guilty of corruption and immorality. Such is the mystery of the Church, that a Divine institution is administered by sinners. Despite the current obsession with 'celebrity', the importance of the pope lies in the office rather than the person. Even the 'bad popes' have safeguarded the deposit of faith and encouraged the mission of the Church.

Along with the bishops, the pope defends the truth of the Gospel and constantly teaches us in the face of indifference, secularism, doubt and scepticism that we encounter in the modern world. We need Peter today just as much as the first followers of Christ. And so let us pray:

Lord Jesus, shelter our Holy Father the Pope under the protection of Thy Sacred Heart. Be Thou his light, his strength and his consolation.

Select Bibliography

Barraclough, Geoffrey *The Medieval Papacy* (1968)

Collins, Roger *Keepers of the Keys of Heaven. A History of the Papacy* (2009)

Duffy, Eamon *Saints and Sinners. A History of the Popes* (1997)

Guarducci, Margherita *The Primacy of the Church of Rome* (2003)

Kelly, J. N. D. *Oxford Dictionary of Popes* (1986)

Maxwell-Stuart, P. G. *Chronicle of the Popes* (1997)

Norman, Edward *The Roman Catholic Church. An Illustrated History* (2007)

Salza, John *The Biblical Basis for the Papacy* (2007)

Walsh, John Evangelist *The Bones of St Peter* (1982)